WHEN TRUE SIMPLICITY IS GAINED

WHEN TRUE SIMPLICITY IS GAINED

*Finding Spiritual Clarity
in a Complex World*

Martin Marty and Micah Marty

WILLIAM B. EERDMANS PUBLISHING COMPANY

GRAND RAPIDS, MICHIGAN / CAMBRIDGE, U.K.

WHEN TRUE SIMPLICITY IS GAINED
Finding Spiritual Clarity in a Complex World

Cover design: Willem Mineur
Separations and printing: Gardner Lithograph, Buena Park, California
The Laser Fultone process is a registered trademark of Gardner Lithograph.

Library of Congress Cataloging-in-Publication Data

Marty, Martin E., 1928–
    When true simplicity is gained / Martin Marty and Micah Marty.
      p.   cm.
    ISBN 0-8028-4237-2 (pbk. : alk. paper)
    1. Simplicity—Religious aspects—Christianity. I. Marty, Micah.
  II. Title.
  BV4647.S48M36   1998
  242—dc21
                                     98-18065
                                       CIP

Manufactured in the U.S.A.

02   01   00   99   98   9 8 7 6 5 4 3 2 1

'Tis the gift to be simple, 'tis the gift to be free,

'Tis the gift to come down where we ought to be,

And when we find ourselves in the place just right,

'Twill be in the valley of love and delight.

When true simplicity is gain'd,

To bow and to bend we shan't be asham'd,

To turn, turn will be our delight

'Till by turning, turning we come round right.

("Simple Gifts," Shaker Gift Song)

Author's Introduction

Simplicity: virtually everyone wants it. Advertisers peddle "the simple life" and consultants help busy people find "the simple way." How-to books on the subject fill library shelves. Individuals go on retreat to find themselves, away from the busy and complex world. At the center of their quest: simplicity.

To deny the urge to simplify life would be to deny much of the spiritual and religious impulse of humanity through the ages. The great religious teachers challenged their disciples to come to the core of things, and that heart and core was simple. Thus Jesus in the Gospels tells would-be disciples that they must become like little children, whose lives, full of trust, would strike them as simple.

Many of the advertised paths to simplicity can be quite complex. As we explored the many writings on the subject, we found that most of them had this in common: they gave us complicated advice on how to live simply. Some of them tell you what thirty things to do each morning to make the day easier. Others ask you to organize your desktop or kitchen, your office drawers and your computer files, all in the interest of making it possible for you to think and act more simply.

If you think I mention all this in order to belittle the quest for simplicity and other means of attaining it, I have been unclear. So brambled, so overgrown, so meandering are the pathways of life that anyone who can find a way through them and along them ought to be cheered. I merely seek to invite you into a different book with a different agenda and a different counsel. Here our goal is to complement the self-help books by treating simplicity as a gift and then asking how we should receive it and the other gifts that come with it.

The photographs in these pages take us to one particular simple place apart and afar from most of us—and bring it into our own places and near to our own hearts. In the American past, any number of communities made efforts to promote the simple way, and here we visually visit one of them, letting it stand for all. Then somewhere in the classic prayers, in scripture readings, and in the quiet of the mind that can come in the face of art, we can begin to be more reposed, more at ease, more ready to take on the challenges of the day and the terrors of the night. For some of us, this will mean becoming more involved with communities—parishes, congregations, classes, and causes—where others are on the same quest. But for all of us, this reflection on gifts that come along with the grace of simplicity should be an aid and, we hope, an occasion for daily enjoyments, if one can reach it on the bedstand, desktop, the table in a breakfast nook, or in one of those briefcases with which we busy people go about living our busy lives.

Martin E. Marty

Photographer's Introduction

French author Antoine de Saint Exupéry defined perfection as that which is achieved "not when nothing more can be added, but when nothing more can be taken away." These words eloquently embody the call of simplicity in photography and art—and in life and faith, as well.

Photography, unlike most other arts, involves at its essence the stripping away of the superfluous. While the painter begins with a blank canvas, to which paint is added, the photographer starts with everything—an infinitely crowded canvas, as it were—and progressively removes various elements. To the photographer, every great scene to be photographed already exists some-where in the world; the challenge lies in deciding where to point the camera and then eliminating from the field of view everything that does not contribute to the desired result.

Taking on the challenge of simplifying our lives follows much the same pattern: we direct our focus to that which is important and eliminate distractions. But this requires us to clarify what is essential. If the virtue of simplicity is that it lets us remove the superfluous clutter and distracting junk from our lives, what do we want to have left over at the end as the focus and center of our lives? When we decide to focus on God, and our faith, simplicity is less difficult to embrace; pushing things out of the way then reveals rather than diverts us from our goal. As a result, we do not have the gnawing sense of giving up things of great value (the consumer culture's definition of simplifying), because what is left in our lives has more appeal and meaning than what was discarded.

For centuries, various religious communities have sought to live the ideal of a simple, God-centered life. Notable among them were the Shakers, a nineteenth-century American movement whose emphasis on simplicity and humility led them to create everyday objects of timeless beauty. While their theology and lifestyle are not what we would choose to follow, images from their world can help us reflect on our own pursuit of a faithful focus. Their aesthetic has become something of a visual shorthand for simplicity, yet it is far enough removed from our own everyday lives to prompt us to think in new and fresh ways about our own pursuit of the simple, God-centered life.

The Shakers would be the first to say that despite all their striving, they could never reach perfection—no more than any humans can. Yet their ability to simplify daily objects and tasks to the point that "nothing more can be taken away" may still evoke in us possibilities and yearnings for how we can live: graced by the gifts of simplicity, community, and faith.

Micah Marty

Notes about the photographs can be found on pages 106–108.

One Day, One Page
One Prayer, One Gift

Ours is a time when so much "spirituality" has become a commodity, something to purchase. Often it is advertised as a product resulting from journeys of the soul taken by isolated seekers. Their leaders, their gurus, invite them to make up their spirituality as they go along. This book offers something different. By drawing upon scriptures and prayers of the community and by referring to the plural, to "us" who seek and find, to author and photographer and reader, we stress that profound spirituality tends to be rooted in particular heritages. Lifelong we plumb scriptures and classic literature and prayer. We draw upon the company of others whom we meet or invite along our way. The more complex this company becomes, the more likely we will be able to see through the complications it represents into the heart of simplicity. That simplicity, in turn and at its depth, is rooted in the very heart of God.

The search for God, with all the heart, need not and does not go on in loneliness. Note that throughout these pages the plural "we" appears far more often than does the singular "I." Even if we are temporarily apart from community, due to travel, illness, or other circumstances, we still draw upon the strength that community provides. Thus nothing has delighted this author and this photographer more than to hear of communal use of our photo-text books — whether in small groups, in worship, at retreats, or over prayer breakfasts.

When True Simplicity Is Gained may well appeal to you if you are in quiet retirement, free to arrange your days as you wish. If your days are long in a senior citizens home, hospital, or hospice, you will find much in these pages on which to draw. If you are heading out for a weekend retreat, take this along and let it speak to you. Or if you cannot clear the calendar and remove all the demanding details that come with daily life, this book is for you, too. Minutes given to it should help one grow in grace and in appreciation of the simple gifts. Meditate upon the suggested Bible reading and the phrase from a classic prayer. Reflect on the facing photograph. Read each meditation title as the completion of the statement "When true simplicity is gained, it brings with it . . ."

Although these forty-seven pairings of photographs and text are suited for any time of year, they take on special meaning in Lent. If you begin reading "a gift a day" on Ash Wednesday, you will find the book climaxes on Easter. Along the way, particular celebrations of the gifts of community and our life within it fall on Sundays, a day of communal gathering. (To help you keep your place, Sundays are marked with an asterisk in "Notes on the Photographs," which begins on page 107.) However and whenever you choose to use this book, we hope it will be for you a time of searching, evaluation, and openness to gifts, a pilgrimage on which we join you and others, guided by the God of grace.

The first lines of the prayers and their authors are on noted pages 109–110.

Attentiveness

*Let not our minds rest upon goods, things, houses, lands,
inventions of vanities, or foolish fashions.*

The gift of simplicity calls for attentiveness to the lasting, the eternal. This does not require that we despise the temporal and the temporary, the things of this world, the gifts that God has given along with the kingdom promised by Christ. Rather it urges us to make the proper distinctions.

A Hasidic story tells of a man who could not make such distinctions. Advised that to achieve paradise he had to shun the "goods" of this world, he avoided good food, good music and art, good company, and good times. Eventually he died. Of course, he had made his goal: he did wake up in paradise. Yet three days later, the angels had to throw him out because the ascetic did not understand or appreciate anything that was happening or provided there.

This kind of story is easy to misuse. It can become a charter for mere worldly attachment. In its spirit, we are tempted to let our minds finally rest on such "goods." We risk losing perspective. Having things such as clothes and works of art, houses to live in, lands whose fruit to enjoy, is to be conceived as a gift of God. Possession is not necessarily a barrier to simplicity—so long as it does not take over one's soul.

Prayers have long given voice to the profound desire for freedom from the less lasting, less important items, the "inventions of vanities or foolish fashions." Immediately attractive, and therefore jarring opposites to the gifts that come with simplicity, these baubles readily become lures that are difficult to pass up. The rewards for passing them by, however, speak for themselves. Such rewards become evident in the lives of those who learn to keep objects in perspective, who thus make up a company that we would like to enter and share.

Colossians 3:12–17

Learning

Teach me, dear Lord, to read clearly this book of life.
I wish to be like a simple child, accepting your word
regardless of whether I understand your purposes.

The gift of simplicity offers opportunities for learning, the way a helpful book does. If we picture our existence as a "book of life," we see ourselves daily writing new pages and chapters simply in the acts of living. Think of the trudging child who totes her lunch pail schoolward. Think then of the toiler who carries an empty lunch pail or a full briefcase homeward. Even in such simple movements we act out sentences in chapters.

These books of lives sometimes look like the assignment books of schoolchildren. This I have accomplished. This I ought to have done, or done better. This I have to do. The lists of assignments are usually too long, the tasks they describe, overly complicated. At the end of the day, as we review the pages, more often than not we are discouraged. Parts of some pages will please us, but the overall record is likely to seem weak. We fear failure again tomorrow. What will the account books of our lives show if we become dispirited?

Sometimes we think the book of life looks like a confusing encyclopedia with a listing of thousands of items in an alphabet that appears scrambled and a language we recognize as foreign. So we consult its Author. "They'll not get God in a book," said a woman who trusted God but mistrusted books. But believers do get *at* God in a book, and we get *at* ourselves by linking our plots with what we can learn of the God plot. Childlike, we review the way these plots link, knowing that the Great Librarian patiently gives us time as we struggle to learn.

Matthew 18:1–5

Focus

Be near to me so that I may not feel the heaviness of labor, nor sink under adversity.

The gift of simplicity can be unburdening, but only if that simplicity comes as a grace and not an achievement. Otherwise, the attempts to lighten life only make its burdens heavier. Such attempts may include visiting bookstores to peruse the shelves of works that tell us how to get rid of complexity. There we find promising tables of contents, with chapter titles that describe the wonders of the life of someone else, a life that had been too complicated but then, thanks to some prescription or formula, was reduced to simplicity.

As we page through the books, glancing at the later chapter titles, the promise of help soon produces a vague uneasiness followed by frustration. Here are "Ten Steps toward Simplicity" of which we are to be mindful. Here are prescriptions for "Thirty Things to Throw Away," since, we are told, we can do without them. These come atop "Twenty Disciplines" and finally "Eleven Basic Thoughts" to keep in mind. Soon wearied, we find that the effort to simplify has only made things more difficult. And worst of all, most of us have employers or customers still to please, students or teachers still to engage. Family members also make proper demands on our time. Our minds become understandably cluttered, and inescapably, our agendas fill.

Over against the busy counsels of the how-to books, quiet prayers are the best defense. However complex our lives, we crave the nearness of the One who can provide us with a present core, a focus for life. Then adversity can only threaten but never overwhelm. The prayer for simplicity produces its surprising yield.

Mark 6:30–31

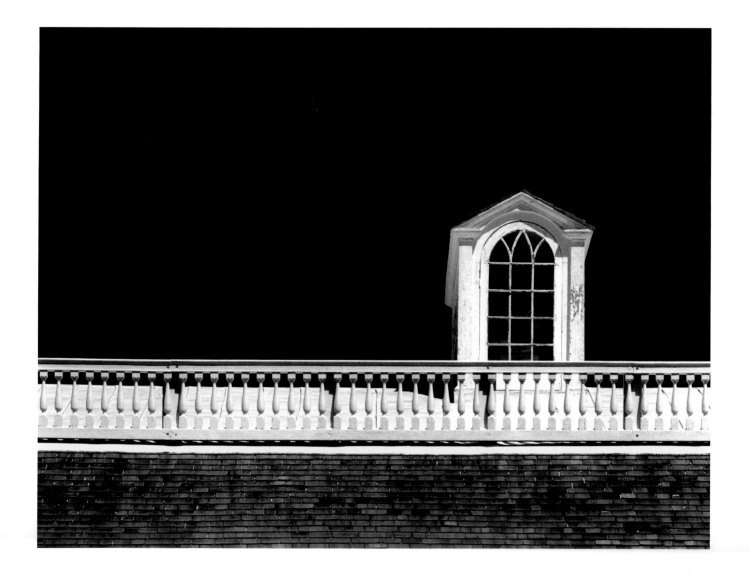

Repose

You made us for yourself,
and our heart is restless until it reposes in you.

The gift of simplicity provides repose. That is the last thing an adolescent desires on a too long, rainy Sunday afternoon. In many homes for aged people where too much quiet living abandons the elderly to boredom, repose does not seem like much of a gift either. They sit back and stare at the hourglass, wherein the sand moves too slowly. Prisoners, whose movements are always limited, until eventually their spirits numbly follow into confinement, shun repose. Boredom leaves the afflicted too distracted for them to be content with superficial simplicity. The senior who waits for a visitor and the prisoner who longs for release live and all but die under the weight of busy, crowded, complex mental agendas.

Whether confinement is forced or not and even while it may distance us from the clutter of objects and the daily confusion of events, it never eases restlessness. Spiritual uneasiness and turmoil do not depend on whether we are here or there, free or not, busy or bored. Forgetting whose we are and for what end humans were created, and toward which they are moved, is instead at the root of unsettledness.

Until we relocate the heart and its quest in God, we can never find life to be simple. All the foods in the spiritual cafeteria seem equally alluring — and equally unfulfilling. Having too many choices strewn throughout the valley of decision stuns us. Jumpily then we move on — unsatisfied and with minds unresolved — to face other choices that seem equally distant or to be tempted to make uninformed decisions. But at the crucial moment, grafted back into the heart of God, human hearts find the true repose that allows them to be creative.

Matthew 11:28–30

19

Community

O God, who hast bound us together in this bundle of life, give us grace to understand how our lives depend upon the courage, the industry, the honesty, and the integrity of our fellow humans; that we may be faithful in our responsibilities to them.

The gift of simplicity builds community. One way to think of our life together is to recall the Roman fasces: the elm or birch twigs drawn together from twisted, tangled piles and tied into a bundle. The fasces was strong because it was bound, and thus it became a symbol of authority. Modern Fascists, alas, took their name, image, and idea from this Latin word for bundle. Yet their negative example of forced commonality does not diminish the promise of this positive reality: we are bound together, and our lives depend upon this bundle called humanity, of which individualists are often unmindful.

Thoughtful breakfasters realize that they benefit from the work of early rising bakers, printers of the newspaper, and those who keep the turbines running so the electric appliances work. Parents sending their children off to school take advantage of the bound-together lives of taxpayers, boards, and teachers. Those who bring spiritual needs and gifts to a congregation gain power to achieve there what they could never have done in isolation.

We recognize the dangers of forced binding and the slackness of some who lack industry and honesty. Yet we also reflect on the way complex energies of those who are, by choice, bound together can simplify the lives of all of us in our mutuality. They lift those of us whom God now calls to become responsible.

1 Corinthians 12:12–26

The Sacred

You have through each day helped me to build a temple of prayer in my heart, so that even in the midst of my labors, I may rejoice in you.

The gift of simplicity turns the profane into the sacred. Here *profane* does not mean vulgar or blasphemous. Instead it refers to that which is *pro*, "outside of," the *fanum*, which is the Latin word for temple. Those who appreciate the grace that comes with simplicity are free to move both ways across the thresholds of the temple each and every day. They bring the beauty of the sacred into ordinary life and ordinary concerns into the holy place.

Believers do not have to travel far to search for this temple of prayer. It goes wherever we go. When we are at home within it, we come and go confidently, facing daily duties and delights. When we are at ease with it, we regularly transact across the threshold of the heart's temple, breathing worded and wordless prayers alike.

The problem—who can always avoid it?—is that when we are in the midst of distractions, we tend to stop transacting. *In the midst of:* we find ourselves distracted by buttoning and unbuttoning clothes with our arthritic fingers; pushing stalled cars; balancing the books; working at the computer or counter; playing; looking up a fact; taking notes; smiling back at the image of a benign saint pictured on the wall or frowning at the reality of a troubling saint next door. Precisely in the midst of our labors, we come to recognize that the temple of prayer is always available. It remains as close as our heart, waiting for us to enter and be refreshed.

Psalm 141:1–2

Wisdom

Give us the true courage that shows itself by gentleness;
the true wisdom that shows itself by simplicity;
and the true power that shows itself by modesty.

The gift of simplicity readies us to revise our ordinary opinions. Before reflecting, we might describe brave persons as bold, brusque, and harsh. Did they not have to be thus if they were to bash the heads of enemies in whose hands they saw the menace of maces and bludgeons? In such habitual ways of thinking, we may well define wisdom as what comes from the storage spaces of a brilliant mind on display and may associate power with the already powerful, potency with those who keep telling us "We're Number One!"

But if we take second thoughts, we ask, Are not the people admired through the ages the ones whose courage outlasted all those possessed of other qualities? Because the truly great selflessly forgot themselves, they help us remember others so we can see the need to be patient and gentle in a world of self-centeredness. As for their wisdom, it inspires us to reshape our lives in the light of examples that reveal no trace of show-off or know-it-all mannerisms.

"Like genius, simple; that is why they are the great teachers," a historian with an encyclopedic mind wrote in dedicating his book to his three children. Yes, like genius, simple: the Imparter of wisdom, who chooses to teach and save the world by means of the gentle, the simple, the modest—as in the case of the helpless, dying Jesus—helps us today discern the wise among the knowing. God breaks down our own harshness, complexity, and immodesty, thus freeing us for others.

John 13:12–15

Peace

Your will is our peace. Deliver me from the false choices that come from self-interest, cowardice, and lack of faith in you, and give me vision and strength to do your will.

The gift of simplicity enables those who welcome it to make precarious choices with some confidence. This day, each day, demanding and beguiling choices confront us. Shall I make this investment or that? Trust this person and distrust that one? Give priority to this assignment or seek another? Visit someone who might need me or steward my energies for some other purpose? Live by hope or let despair take over?

Not to decide, we know, is to decide. Even whether to make a choice demands choice. A wit of our time offers bizarre counsel: "My advice is, when you come to a fork in the road, take it." Take it? If so, then which fork? Since the book of the future is closed, we seek to minimize the number of bad optings and to choose with some confidence among promising alternatives. Serious people learn to gain perspective on the choices they must make from the experience and knowledge they possess.

The voice of *true* simplicity prompts us to discern the foolishness of looking out only for ourselves and thus overlooking both the common good and our own human limits. Abraham Lincoln taught about limits: "The purposes of the Almighty are perfect, and must prevail, though we erring mortals may fail to accurately perceive them in advance." The divine will does not impart secrets of the future. Still and wisely we say with all others who have responded to it, in that will is our peace.

Ephesians 1:9–23

Imagination

Let no little ends or low imagination stain our spirit,
or profane any of our words and actions.

The gift of simplicity enlivens; it never dulls imagination. Lower your
sights and idle your mental motor, some counselors urge those who seek
a simpler life. Yet such lowering of sights does not bring clarity to vision.
The downcast eye falls on beer cans and sidewalk cracks, on crawling things
and junk piles, but fails to look at wonders above. It ignores the singular sun
and the open sky.

The busy imagination produces complexity. So it is said. Of course, if the
imagination has no starting or ending point it *will* produce only confusion.
Then we describe it as "low." However, if a person remains aware that imagination has been built into the creature by the Creator and that what it brings
to mind can serve us in the acts of creation, there come into play higher imagination and larger ends.

Convince people that the chessboard offers more options for moves than
there are believed to be neutrons in our universe and they may ask, Given
such choices, why must I then plagiarize lines for my poems or dully "follow
the lines" when Sunday-painting? Why not sketch what I see or think and
improvise? When there is no hindrance, people do follow the imagination into
greater ends and heights. Simply, a person then completes the contract, applies
the paint, caresses the loved one, and arranges the list of things to do for this
day, or the next, and does them.

Job 38:4–11

Freedom

Old habits that I cannot throw off, old customs
that are so much a part of my life that I am helpless:
give me strength to break the bonds;
give me courage to live a new life in you.

The gift of simplicity helps us see what would imprison us. Perhaps not visible handcuffs, shackles, or prison doors—only a few of us have to contend with those today. What imprisons may instead be invisible, or it may be so close to us that we do not notice the power of its grip. What the naked eye cannot see, the naked soul learns to discern.

That bare soul, stripped of its blinders and liberated from its own binding pretenses, reveals how bound and paralyzed by the power of habit and custom we can be. Some prayers speak of these habits and customs as being old. If we do something new and do it only once, there is seldom an automatic impulse to repeat it. But if we do something a thousand times, it is hard *not* to repeat it. The fresh resolves that we make on New Year's Days and birthdays but soon forget and the repentances we may express seem weak against the binding force of what we have done so frequently. What we do so habitually often creates illusions of security and holds us captive.

Some old habits and customs, to be sure, *can* serve the purposes of God. Thus we learn to be stewards, becoming habitually generous. Yet other old habits can continue to block God's purposes. As if addicted, we may eat or drink, inhale or inject, the wrong substances. In such a course of dependent life, we will come to feel defeated. But in the company of supportive and challenging people and under the tutelage of God the liberator, all of our closest enemies—which means our own old ways—can begin to be defeated, and we become newly free.

Romans 7:14–25

Thresholds

*Make the threshold of this house smooth enough to be
no stumbling block to children, nor to straying feet, but
rugged and strong enough to turn back the tempter's power.*

The gift of simplicity resembles the plan of the builder, the work of the carpenter. It helps us order the elements that make our day and provides the foundation for living, the framework for deciding. Among these elements are windows that let in the light and doors that can be opened for receiving the neighbor but closed for protection from the enemy. The door's threshold can serve as a figure for actual ways of living.

Who has never stumbled over ridges on a threshold, one designed to air-seal a room when the door is closed yet creating a danger when it is open? Children have stumbled. On the other hand, the termite-ridden, decayed, or weakly built threshold will eventually crash. It can no longer be part of a protection system. From unsmooth thresholds, the bare feet of the poor stranger pick up splinters.

The threshold comes to stand for the comings and goings of people throughout the days and years. It suggests the heart that can put up barriers against the guests who should be welcome or the heart that can produce no barriers against the enemies who would destroy. Fixed in our mind as the image for this day, the threshold prompts us to measure those comings and goings in a new way. Living is simple when the threshold is smooth enough for the innocent to cross and enter our lives and strong enough to bar the beguilers. God rightly frames the door to our souls and our lives as promised, and friend and neighbor freely cross its threshold.

Ephesians 2:19–22

Church

*Grant that the course of this world may be so peaceably
ordered by thy governance, that thy Church may joyfully
serve thee in all godly quietness.*

The gift of simplicity is the gift of life together with fellow believers.
These years an explosion of personal and self-invented spirituality marks
our society. Usually it takes the form of highly individual seeking and of sacred
journeys pursued by souls in isolation. It results in the fashioning and following
of life courses that people tailor only for themselves, designed for personal
development unmatched and untouched by that of others.

In that culture we overhear a prayer that drops the words "thy Church."
This shocks, this offends: to many, *church* means institution, organization,
bureaucracy, the gathering of the dull, the inhibitor of spiritual development,
and sometimes even the abuser of the unprotected. All those meanings and
images can be connected with *the* church, as it is listed in the phone book,
advertised in the papers, described in negative news reports.

Today, however, we pray instead for *thy* Church, which is a very different
matter. This "thy Church" is born of the fire of divine inspiration, fused
with the sacrifices of inspired people called saints, and embodied in the lives
of a billion and more living people. All of them are capable of warring, and
none of them naturally adheres to the divine ordering and governing of things.
Naturally.

The "thy Church" then receives the simple gifts, not least among which is joy,
the joy of serving. Such service does not mean the end of adventure, but it
does offer quietness of spirit to all, to each, to us.

Acts 10:34–36

Blitheness

As the day brings us the petty round of irritating duties,
help us perform them with laughter and kind faces;
give us to go blithely on our business.

The gift of simplicity does not replace the many duties of the day, but it counters the irritations that can come with them. *Can* come? They *do* come, say frank friends, who ask us to "get real" if we boast of holding positions that are always and only fulfilling. Come on, urge practical-minded persons who recognize that even exciting assignments involve drudgeries. Fill out these forms. Follow these steps. Write these recommendations. Do this laundry. Grade these papers. Wait for latecomers. Add yet one more task at 7 P.M. before taking the rest of the day off. Duties irritate.

An observer ponders, Why are some people thrown off by irritations while others remain lighthearted about them? Why do some stagger under the burden of duty, while others carry it lightly? A complainer asks, Why am I on some days done in by the drudgeries while on others I am able to laugh at a long and hopelessly demanding agenda?

In the house of God's simplicity, the answers to those questions will always address the fact that it is not the length of our petty rounds or our lists of things to do that makes life so hard to simplify. The lesson is clear: if the spirit with which we greet the day's details is serene, the challenges of the day will not be daunting. Rather than paste on an artificial smile and grimly set about our work, we learn to laugh defiantly when the lists and agendas are long — and to keep a perspective that allows blitheness to develop and to color the actions of the day.

1 Peter 5:6–7

Dazzlement

*Lord, you are like a wildflower. You spring up in places where
we least expect you. The bright color of your grace dazzles us.
Far from trying to possess you, may you possess us.*

The gift of simplicity overturns what we have expected. The cactus lover
tensely watches the night-blooming cereus she has tenderly nurtured
indoors, but it sometimes disappoints her, holding back its fragrant secret or
letting its flower too quickly fall. Then, realizing that her expectations have
gone unmet, she takes a fresh and longer look outside at the dawn. Beyond the
window a desert blossoms, and wildflowers defy the barren sandscape.

Expectation often keeps us busy and forces us to fuss over everything that we
plant and cultivate, work and do, harvest and store. Well and good: the garden
of life needs cultivators and reapers. But the busy, fussy gardener can overlook
the wild beauty that comes on its own and simply amazes. When the time comes
for grace to be discerned, this divine grace draws the eye away from the tended
pot where a meager and momentary bloom would have been. Grace pulls our
attention instead to the colors or fragrances that arrive without our effort,
by the Creator's activity.

The sense of duty, of course, calls us to be responsible: to plant, to snip and
prune, to nurture and watch what grows. But duty needs a context. Left to
itself, obligation takes over life and preoccupies the mind of the dutiful.
Needing and reaching for help when facing the call of duty, we may be tempted
to grasp greedily for whatever is at hand, to want to possess it—and still to
name it "grace." But if "grace" is thus seized, it loses its power to surprise.
Divine grace, instead, possesses the free person. It comes in the name of
the Lord of the unexpected, the one who chooses to dazzle the weary in
our otherwise dulling gray field of vision.

John 4:7–15

Strength

We beseech you to deliver us from the fear of the unknown future; from fear of failure; from fear of poverty; from fear of bereavement; from fear of loneliness; from fear of sickness and pain; from fear of age; and from fear of death.

The gift of simplicity lifts fear from our future. Usually we store away, far back in the recesses of the mind, Jesus' words to take no thought for tomorrow since God lives there and will care for us. We shelve the assurance "Fear not, I am with you" in mental storage bins. Understandably more vivid are the complications of the doings or the to-be-dones of today and tomorrow.

Almost all of the days' agendas induce fear when they are related to the anxious "I." Will I make the sale or make the grade—or will I fail? Will my insurance and pension hold out? Will I keep my once secure job? Will that lump on the side of my throat be cancerous? Will I endure the heartache my children or my spouse may cause? Will I cause their hearts to ache? Will I lose my powers and resources as the diminishments of aging work their way and the shadows lengthen? Will I be given strength to face death in anticipation of victory?

Trust no one who claims to have no fears. Off guard and unguarded in quiet late-night conversations, even those apparently most self-assured and in command confess to such anxieties. These all connect with the unknown. The simple gifts, however, deal with what *can* be known about the future, a knowing that lifts and guides us today: Jesus, who told us not to be anxious, gave us reason not to be. A God who loves us is the power of the future.

Matthew 6:25–34

Company

Give us the spirit of charity in all our dealings with our fellows, and the spirit of gaiety, courage, and a quiet mind in facing all tasks and responsibilities.

The gift of simplicity rarely summons us *away from* community. True, some people have felt called to desert the crossroads, the places of connection and commotion, to head for the desert or the cell. There, undistracted, they find in prayer an uncluttered communication of soul and God. For everyone else, the call is *into* community.

In company we often meet people who at first jar us, because they are abrasive. They disturb us, because their personalities do not match ours. They make us want to scream and lead us to agonize, because their prescriptions and scoldings violate the serenity we think we would find if they had never come close to us.

The call to true community is a call to the spirit of charity. Charity, if gaily pursued, leads us to say "Aha!" where for a long time we had been blinded because of captivity to selfishness. Charity, courageously pursued, helps us overcome the timidity resulting from the lack of practice at dealing with others. Charity, if quietly acted upon, makes it easier to sort out trivial tasks from true ones, self-centered pursuits from those that may bring us closer to harmony with strangers who then become fellows.

The solitary monk who prays in the desert, the contemplative nun in the cell, may well serve divine purposes. But it is in the world of action that we are to be envied: there we greet the opportunities that interaction with others always brings.

Colossians 2:6–7

Lodging

May he support us all the day long, till the shades lengthen,
and the evening comes, and the busy world is hushed,
and the fever of life is over, and our work is done!
Then in his mercy may he give us a safe lodging,
and a holy rest, and peace at the last.

The gift of simplicity makes us attentive to language, but not in the way that grammarians or writers of dictionaries have to be. Instead it encourages us to listen for both the stirring sounds of life and for the silences that follow the use of calming phrases.

Lovers of prose now and then play the game of pointing to instances in which someone uses language well. Not a few will nominate this elegant prayer by John Henry Newman as among the most beautiful sentences in the English language. Millions have voiced it at evening worship or breathed it as a bedtime word before God, the merciful one. They, we, have found that praying it simplifies understandings of what the day is about and provides calm in the face of the terrors of the night.

What works well at evening, when the spent day offers no more challenges than for us to yield everything back to divine Mercy, also can guide the pilgrim through the day. In the morning, we think of "the day long" with all its complications. In early afternoon, the shades of frustration begin to grow: so much has been left undone. The hushing of the world, the lowering of life's fever, the freedom to yield the tedium of the long hours can be prospects all the day. Beyond all this lies the greater prospect of safe lodging and the peace that comes with it.

Psalm 4:8

Priority

*Let my first thought today be of thee, let my first impulse
be to worship thee, let my first speech be thy name,
let my first action be to kneel before thee in prayer.*

The gift of simplicity lets us depart from a natural way of starting the day: feeling burdened with cares. Contributing to that weight, the first thought of the day may dwell on guilt carried over from yesterday. Such thoughts loom as uncreative, but they are hard to displace. The first impulse for anyone may be to worry about the day's agenda: there are many complex items to tackle and many complications to cause stress. The first speech of the day, as often as not, is a grumble about sniffles or aches or insomnia or against a family member who did not turn on the coffeepot or who made too much predawn noise. The first action tends to be routine and practical: a reach for the shower handle, the shaver, the cosmetic bag, or the daily newspaper.

So much for the natural, the almost inevitable, the apparently urgent things that take over, if we let them. Beginning today, we reach for a different concept, an almost *super*natural grasp of the gifts that are ours if we are open to them. We try out this act of receiving, and the day turns out differently. We let our minds be fixed on the Thou who purges guilt, urges us not to let worry dominate, and inspires the language of prayer, language which makes grouching irrelevant. The practical action of the day follows. We still might do what we knew we had to do, but we are now free to direct action to higher purpose.

Psalm 108:1–4

51

Lightness

Turn my soul into a garden, where the flowers dance
in the gentle breeze, praising you with their beauty.
Let my soul be filled with beautiful virtues.

The gift of simplicity displaces the ugly and selfish impulses of the soul that accepts it. Those of us who studied physics learned that displacement refers to the weight or volume of a fluid that gives way when a floating object, such as a boat or a cork, is placed in it. Thus, one weight gives way to the other.

Picture the heavy, complicated soul burdened with its mixture of vices and virtues and weighted by both ugliness and beauty, by evil elements that pull us from God and also by attractions that draw us Godward. A seeker of God will dream of a soul from which these vices and ugliness are somehow displaced by virtue and beauty, by essentials. When ancient writers of prayers thought of beauty, they often spoke of lightness, of tended gardens full of delicate blossoming flowers. If we too think in their terms, we learn to replace the heavy and weighting images with those of airiness and freedom.

When the prayer makers thought of the soul as a garden, they liked to picture in it the Creator setting a breeze into motion and the flowers of the soul to dancing. On a gray morning or a dark night, in late autumn or in barren years as much as in brighter times, the imagination of such dancing signals that divine activity is all around us, only waiting to be recognized. The prayer and the dream that goodness might displace everything that was flawed in the soul come to be realized for another dancing day.

Hebrews 12:1–2

Discernment

God, give us grace to accept with serenity the things that cannot be changed, courage to change the things that should be changed, and the wisdom to distinguish the one from the other.

The gift of simplicity imparts to us the ability to make distinctions. On familiar landscapes we are less likely than elsewhere to notice the widening of fissures along fault lines. While we ought to act to avoid them, we often may ignore the signals or find ourselves unmotivated to discern when to take them seriously enough to move around and beyond them.

Then any day, one like today, some things occur that prompt new motives for us to distinguish and act. In the twenty-four hours ahead, the most difficult and complicating of these will not have to do with hitherto unrecognized danger signs in the external landscape but with what we might call the innerscape, with the fault lines of the soul. Thus the alcoholic, whose company we share or who we are, is drawn up short when someone at last has the courage to call him to surrender or convince her that she is existing at the edge of the abyss. Some who respond become Alcoholics Anonymous, in whose company they pray today's Serenity Prayer. Voicing it is a call for grace to distinguish.

The addicted learn, as do all self-examiners, that everyone has to deal with an inherited genetic package and the experiences that have seared the mind. We cannot do much to change our character, but we are graced to distinguish between what we inherit or do by habit and what we can change or will find altered by God, the agent of change, who never abandons us to the changelessness that would by itself blind and dull us.

Luke 19:1–10

Creation

Guide me to find my rightful place in your creation, that in some small way I may add to the beauty of your handiwork.

The gift of simplicity charters a license to create. In the context of such creativity, however, no one is called to be Prometheus. That hero stole fire from the gods, but in his arrogance, he came to a bad end—after thirty thousand years of dangling in suffering—and was unable to do good for any of his fellows. Neither is one gifted or called to become a foolish and dangerous god-man of the kind philosopher Friedrich Nietzsche pursued. Nor is one urged to follow the American figure described as "a self-made man who worshiped his creator."

Instead, creative gifts are freed when we are given, and then find, a place within the patterns and anticipations of divine creation. Being in such a position does not dull the imagination. Recalling names such as Rembrandt, Bach, and Milton suggests how much shaping power is turned loose among people who want only to add to the beauty of the divine handiwork.

Now it is possible, *just* possible, that one or another of us may wake up today recognizing within ourselves a hitherto undiscovered genius to match that of the artists mentioned. But most of us know that our place lies in the company of ordinary people who do what they can with ordinary days. Such knowing is liberating. It frees parents who get to be in on the creation of a developing child. They have daily opportunities to create, opportunities displayed through their signals of affection and discipline. They are permitted further to beautify the divine handiwork that is their share in the human race. In Christ we become new creations. Whether then we teach or endure or earn or cook or dance or cry or pray, we get to take our rightful place and leave behind some new mark of beauty.

Philippians 4:4–9

Presence

Above all let me live in your presence. Let every day
combine the beauty of spring, the brightness of summer,
the abundance of autumn, and the repose of winter.

The gift of simplicity brings change in the midst of continuity. It does not bring the mere and constant change that can unsettle and devastate the spirit, but instead that which overcomes the mere and constant sameness that can numb and induce boredom. Those who live in zones where seasons change drastically do well to let the changes signal both differing gifts and possibilities as well as a need for the warmth and vitality of cherished continuity.

Climate control, we call it: we chop and burn the wood or turn up the thermostat for warmth in winter. In summer we ice the water and turn down the thermostat to cool the air. Busily we twist and turn dials, open and close windows and shutters, and change apparel to adjust to the two intervening seasons.

Doing all this permits some of the beauty and brightness, the abundance and repose of the four seasons to be enjoyed year-round. But can one own this beauty, and only this, daily? Not in any simple way. Millions have suffered physically from the floods of spring, the drought of summer, the famine of fall, and the violence of winter. Spiritually, people suffer as well.

The One who sets the seasons, however, comes as a presence through each of them. Where we choose to ignore that presence, change devastates or sameness upsets. Where that presence is realized, each day makes available for our receiving a goodness that mixes change and continuity in all seasons of weather, for all seasons of the soul.

Job 37:5–13

Purification

You wove the tapestry of life.
Make us clean with the strong soap of your truth.

The gift of simplicity satisfies a hunger for purity. We move through this day and walk through tomorrow in a milieu that is graffitied with smudges and smears. These can result routinely from the disarrays of nature, as when mud washes up on wave-cleansed sand. A patient eye then lets nature find its course and take its time to effect natural cleaning action.

Most stains and blots we know result not from natural processes but from the violations of the spiritual landscape that follow from human choices. The days are then marked by our sense of uneasiness and sometimes guilt, products of what we choose to do when we rub against the benign purposes of creation. Developed as we are out of the hard-to-plot genetic strands with which our ancestors endowed us, we speak of the weavings of God. These are the criss-crossings of threads out of which the garment or the tapestry of life appears. Distinctive, even unique patternings, one per person, mark each of us.

Making sense, making even bits of sense, of the tapestry thus woven is written into the script for each day. We often find it difficult to recognize that sense through the figurative dust and marks on the fabric. Its design, however, becomes partly clear when it is cleansed. Some human acts of discipline play their part in the washings. But richer than such action is the experience of letting the self be purified. This cleansing occurs when prayers are said and answered and when we who pray rise from our knees to explore and find some patterns again in that tapestry called life.

Psalm 51:1–7

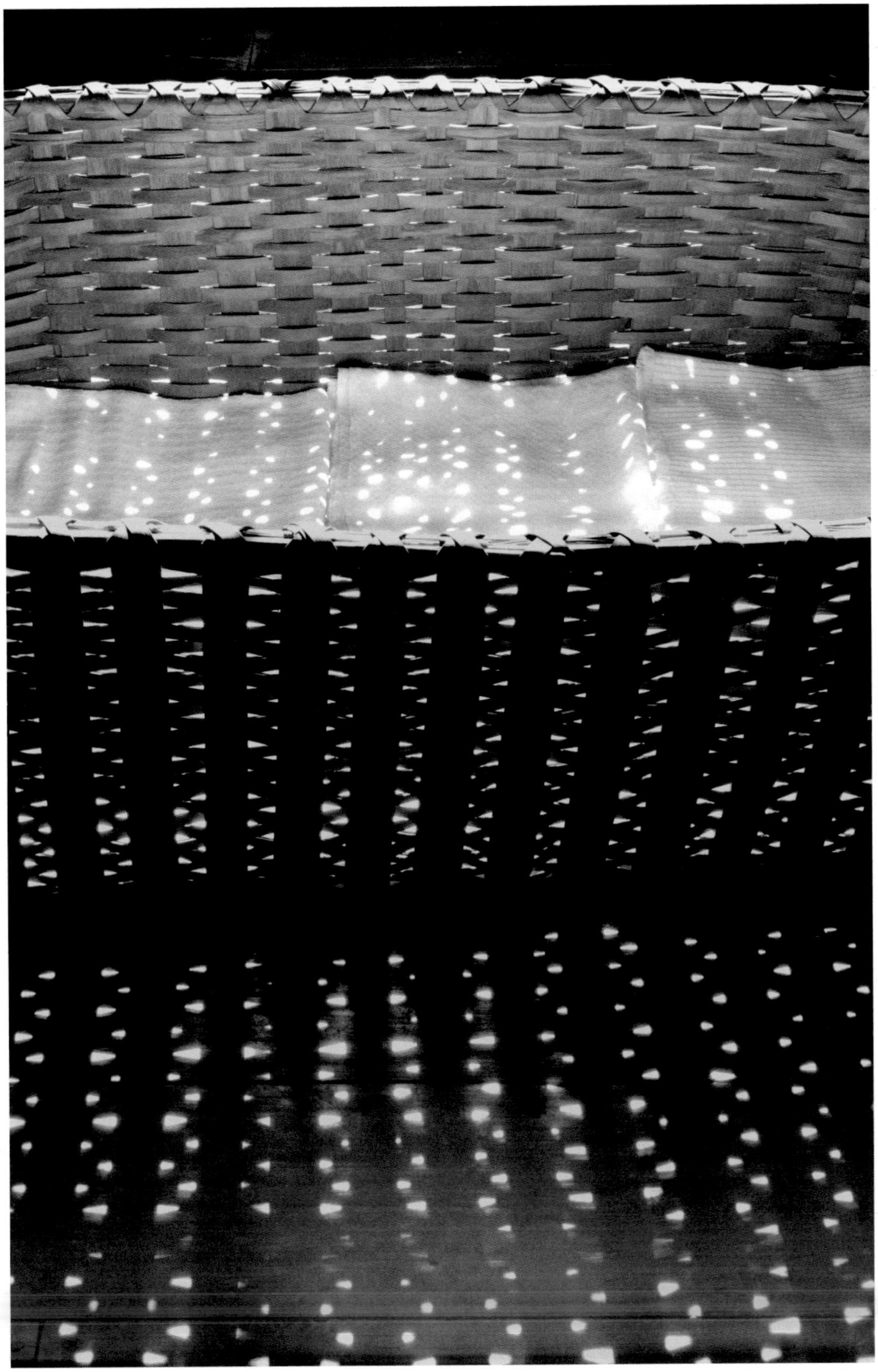

Confidence

As the rain hides the stars, as the autumn mist hides
the hills, as the clouds veil the blue of the sky, so the dark
happenings of my lot hide the shining of your face from me.
Yet, if I may hold your hand in the darkness, it is enough.

The gift of simplicity inspires confidence when stumblers need it most. Believers often picture the courses of their years and days as a walk — one that no one completes without ever being frightened, losing the way, or faltering. Stumblers eventually learn not to try going it alone at all times. Human company is at hand: others before us have struggled through a rain of rage against God or have puzzled in the mist of doubts. Those who have had to wait for the clouds of their own disappointment to clear have something to teach the discouraged wanderers about the eventual, if partial, shining of the divine face upon them.

Honest pathfinders tell us, and they ever will, that the shining presence is not always recognized. The divine companionship is not always intensely realized. But they also assure us that they had been given sufficient guidance and light to go on. We gain from them some new ways of approach to midnight. At such an hour, when darkness thickens, our overbusy and troubled minds tend to forget the starry magnificences, until we come to risk confidence in God, the shaper of the vast spaces. At noon the same minds, our own, often become lost in the palpable, if temporary, mists that appear when the sun of life is hidden. The gift of prayer best makes its point precisely then, because the one who voices it in faith knows that repose in the hand of God suffices.

Psalm 139:1–14

Interaction

Lord, lift us out of private-mindedness and give us public souls to work for your kingdom by daily creating that atmosphere of a happy temper and generous heart which alone can bring the great peace.

The gift of simplicity ensures privacy but not private-mindedness. True, few who seek the simple way will find it without taking some time apart. That time might be during a night when a spirit of repose takes over where insomnia had threatened. Some people welcome the chance to be enclosed in the private capsule of their car, when soothing radio music helps the spirit of a driver rise above the gnarling gridlock. Many set aside a special room, a corner of a library, a place where the curtain can be drawn before they open a book. In such private places and times, seekers deepen their minds.

Private-mindedness, on the other hand, can create illusions. It lets a person think that that bedroom, that driver's seat, that cozy room apart, allows the mind to do true justice to reality. It is possible to make an idol out of a place and time. It is also tempting for the person occupying a place apart and preoccupied during the time alone to turn selfish. Freedom from such idolatry and selfishness opens the soul to others, to the public.

God would meet us in the public realm. There prophets spoke and Jesus walked. There many of the saints were and are at home. The public is where the strangers meet us and stand in the way. There they parade their banners, which do not always match ours. The public is where a jangle of voices and a jumble of causes may result in conflict and disturb our peace. Still the public stage beckons. On it the Lord provides public-minded souls with gifts of a temper and heart that succeed in recognizing the Great Peace when it breaks out into our midst. This can happen today.

Matthew 6:1–7 and Matthew 5:6–13

Perspective

What a being is ours? Obliged to reduce our aim
to a simple view of the little part we fill,
and in quiet acceptance insure tranquility.

The gift of simplicity is not designed to reduce arrogant humans to nothing-ness, but it does equip us to have a better feeling for proportion. In the language of some mystics, humans are called to become Nothing in the face of the Everything, the All, the One. In the language of modern astrophysicists, speck-sized people seem to be dwarfed to the point of becoming absent. These scientists train hyperpowered telescopes on the skies and then announce the potential for discovering there hundreds of billions of new galaxies. In that perspective, individuals appear to have almost no being.

Yet the nonmystical moments of the most prosaic of us, who may lack the astro-physicist's eye and brain, convince us to recognize how significant we are. We are left to seek only perspective. The sense of being small and insignificant, say some, should be the goal in the quest for simplicity. They counsel that thinking too much of the self is the best—or worst—way to make life more confusing and complex than before. It makes us keep on bluffing, creating pretenses, and living up to the self-publicity we generated while puffing up ourselves.

Instead, littleness is ours, but it is never *mere* littleness. It comes in the form of a weakness that brings strength, a weakness we have seen as power in our infant Lord. This child, when grown to adulthood, challenged believers to attempt the heroic, to feel worthwhile enough to make a gift of themselves and of their time for the benefit of others. Perspective for such a resolve comes today when we see that in the puzzling schemes of things we each have some part to fill. It is a part of that whole in which divine peace brings its promise and where the spirit finds tranquility.

Philippians 2:5–8

Change

May I know thee more clearly, love thee more dearly,
and follow thee more nearly: for ever and ever.

The gift of simplicity never comes with a promise that all mysteries will be made clear. If only we could instantaneously see clearly and reach goals unmistakably and immediately. So we dream. In another dream we could this minute let go of lesser loyalties. Thereupon, also at once, we would be able to assert and be aware of total and complete love between God and ourselves, between ourselves and others. If only we could find footing, away from the sands through which we daily slog or the mud which often mires us, so that we would follow the right path. There, we think, it would be easy to be close to the God who calls.

Never, or almost never, is change instantaneous, total, and unmistakable. Instead, simplicity beckons us with words like "more" instead of "most." The life of the disciple of Christ is often measured by comparatives instead of superlatives, by incremental steps not utopian dreams. The dictionary helps us out here: *incremental* means "with slight, often barely perceptible augmentation."

Yet, even if it is only "barely perceptible," the change is perceptible. Today, then, the focus of the eyes of faith will lead us to contentment when we come to see God "more clearly." The heart's response of love is satisfied when we come to love God "more dearly." And the foot's following on the path of hope becomes more sure when we follow God "more nearly." "More" does not mean "the same" or "less"—so we delight in the progress we experience.

1 Corinthians 13:11–12

Openness

Lord, grant me a simple, kind, open, believing, loving, and generous heart, worthy of being your dwelling-place.

The gift of simplicity enables the heart to open and permits us to explore what is within. What is this heart of which we speak? Not the pulsing, pumping physical organ, though of course we care for and about it. Here the word *heart* names our inward being. It stands for all that we are, for all that matters.

In many lives that heart becomes closed as readily as it might have been opened. Such a heart can be clenched like a fist. It may be tensed and hard, so that with it one can strike at others more effectively. It may be tight, so as to hold what it thinks it owns and fears losing. This closed heart can never relax, can never allow its owner to play or laugh, to stretch or caress. Intended to be open, it gets slammed shut and locked. Its householder becomes anxious, guards the little that is within it, and contributes to suspicion of strangers.

Unclenched, the heart opens, becoming like a house with its door ajar as a signal that others are welcome. Then its owner is ready for change, for surprise. She is ready to deal with the conglomerations we call daily life.

Who can risk living with an open door? Those who feel secure, who know that within their very heart there abides constantly the strong and generous Builder of each house, who stays in them and there dwells permanently. Householders with such open doors come to share some qualities with God the builder. They are free to be generous and kind, alert to others who pass by and are welcomed.

Ephesians 3:14–19

Sufficiency

Give me the love of you only, with your grace, and I am rich enough; nor ask I anything beside.

The gift of simplicity frees us from obsession with things. In a vivid gospel word, Jesus tells the disciples to travel light. Heavy luggage and surplus clothing got in the way of their response. One young man was asked to give away his possessions. A rich man who stored his bags of grain in ever bigger barns was called a fool for getting his priorities wrong and his securities from the wrong place.

Some followers of the gospel movements and stories fast or swear vows of poverty in their attempt to to be disciples. Most believers, and many of us among them, act differently. We revere a Creator who causes fields to produce grain and counsels us on how to store and use the products of the field and stream. But always there is a sense of proportion: piling up riches, things, and commodities keeps us very busy. With them we are kept busy counting, protecting, and working to get more and more.

True simplicity does not ask us to throw away all things but to understand their source and, by concentrating on the grace of the Spirit, to be free of the hold that piled-up possessions can have on hearts. Then we can see, no longer blinded by the distracting glitter of things. Divine love is so compelling, divine grace is so rewarding, that to experience them is to find that everything else pales—or appears in a new light.

Luke 12:15–21

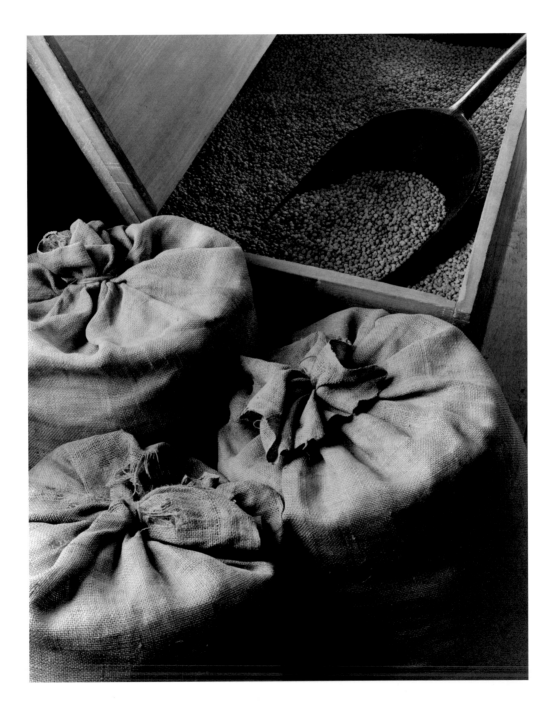

Steadiness

Grant me to design only what is lawful and right;
and afford me calmness of mind, and steadiness of
purpose, that I may do your will in this short life.

The gift of simplicity brings steadiness. Today the lure to waver may be more alluring than the assignment to be steady. While people admire steady performers, they also pay to see sensationally unpredictable entertainers or players. Audiences say they revere the even-tempered, but they especially remember the excitable. Yet, although publics may welcome erratic and stormy performers, they need leaders who stay the course and keep true purposes in view.

Much of the time, particularly in periods of luxury or when people can afford to be superficial, the lure of the unpredictable is satisfying. But further reflection on our own experience reminds us that in the storm of sea or snow we profitably direct confidence to those who have but one thing in mind: finding the destination and getting us there. Most medical breakthroughs come not from charismatic individuals who stumble upon an agent of cure and then romp off to dance the night away. Instead human goods like those of researchers most often emerge because people stayed with their business.

Steadiness by itself is boring. Plodders and dullards display it but achieve little. Steadiness of purpose—assuming our purposes to be true—disciplines us on the meandering paths of our lives. Because true purposes are congruent with divine will, they help launch us when faced with the uncertainty that comes with this day and its night. We can pursue those purposes single-mindedly because of the true promises of the One who calls us to be calm as we follow.

Matthew 14:25–33

Significance

Grant that we may realize that it is the
little things of life that create differences,
that in the big things of life, we are as one.

The gift of simplicity helps people sort out the significant irritations from the insignificant, the little problems from the large. It may also help us discern a half-truth within a prayer so that we might ask for the whole truth that lies behind it. Then we can pray and receive as we ought.

That we are as one in the big things of life is a half-truth. It is hard to get people to agree on many big things that they call absolutes. Yet millions may agree on relatively little things, such as their choice of product brands. With the half-truths safely located, the greater truths stare, and we stare back.

Yet it is true—isn't it true?—that believers are as one in their awareness that God is love; that Christians all affirm that God's love comes through the gift of Jesus Christ; that the Holy Spirit seals that love. It is true—isn't it true?—that it is the little things that come along with our various traditions, regions, habits, and tastes that create the nasty differences.

Whatever a billion other believers around the world do, we each have our own little days and ways among them cut out for us. Isn't it true—it is!—that marital counselors have to guide the energy of couples into overcoming irritating habits so that the original and deeper love, on which they have been as one, gets its chance to win. It is true that each of us will grow stronger, more serene, if today we see through and beyond little irritations and trivia while pursuing the hopes that unite great parts of the human family.

Ephesians 4:1–6

Refuge

Be unto us a comfort on the way, a shade in the heat,
a shelter in trouble, a staff upon uncertain ground.

The gift of simplicity helps those who receive it to weather varieties of circumstances. Those who testify to its benefits like to use language associated with weather. The complex life bewilders those of us who stare at its maps that show many ways of being—until simplicity helps us find *the* way. But then it becomes evident that storms still loom and extremes still threaten along that path.

Today or tomorrow we are likely to be confused by too many commands. Some of us will feel the heat of demands from the boss, the teacher, the spouse, or from the pressures that come from assignments we give ourselves. In that heat, God appears as shade.

Storms arrive. The earth trembles under us in the form of doubt. The clouds of despair gather. The whirlwind and the freezing blast would leave us unprotected. But just when an evil end could result, a promised shelter is realized in the form of the divine love that warms.

Tomorrow, or even today, crags of challenge and hills of exaction will rise in the face of little children of whom much is expected and of seniors who expect too much of themselves. The weary "need a lift" and a means of transport arrives. But circumstances of the day will still throw trouble their way. What to do about that trouble is the live issue. The uncertainties that come with the day diminish when we find refuge from whatever it is that the worst can bring. The One who, we already know, has come as the Good Shepherd also offers his staff on which to lean. With it as security, we walk on what had been uncertain ground with our henceforth more sure steps.

Psalm 121

Grace

May every temporal grace be matched by spiritual grace,
that in both body and soul we may live to your glory.

The gift of simplicity is, simply, the gift of grace, gracefully received. True simplicity is gained not when we outcompete our colleagues in the market, outshoot our teammates on the athletic floor, or outboast our rivals. The competitor, shooter, and boaster lead extremely distracted lives. They have become overbusy keeping up appearances or issuing—and then believing—their self-promoting publicity.

Wipe the mental slate clean of the images of all such strivers. In their place will appear a gallery of graced people, through whom divine glory gets to light up the human parade. We have seen such gracing in the face of anyone who, raging against the closing in of terminal illness, also affirms the day that each rising sun provides. We have recognized this grace in the adolescents who are discovering their potential but are not becoming prideful. We have even been privileged to glimpse it in the mirror on days full of grace, not pretension.

Often in the history of belief we have become aware of people who artificially divide the temporal from the spiritual, their body from their soul. But grace unites. Grace permits no day on the calendar, no hour of the day, to be seen either as only temporal and external—*or* only spiritual and unconnected with human tears and sweat. The divine glory, dazzling and inviting, shines through the graced lives of the least suspecting, of us, among them.

Matthew 5:14–16

Desire

What will befall us today, O God, we know not; we only know that nothing will happen which thou hast not foreseen, determined, desired, and ordered.

The gift of simplicity does not include a promise that we will know in advance everything the day can bring. To foresee the value of stocks on the market would, of course, be profitable. To know what lies ahead would help us fit our feet into the footprints on the path of daily walks. Yet to be able to read fully the plot of what God would detail for the future would necessarily turn humans into robots. To recognize ahead of time the order and ordering of the day's confusions would seem efficient, but it makes the task of living out each day meaningless.

Honestly now: don't we usually think it would be clarifying to know *more* of what might be divinely foreseen, determined, desired, and ordered? Frustrated by the limits of life, infuriated by circumstances that confuse the plot of daily living, we may be tempted to wish for a God who prematurely puts the cards of life on the table for all to read at even a casual glance.

Yet such wishing demands energies that are better put to work on other tasks. Today is one more twenty-four hour period in which we know nothing in detail of what has been divinely foreseen. Little of that has been determined in advance. The longer we linger on the theme—instead of the unknown particulars—of the day's futures, however, the surer we are of knowing what God desires, until we desire the same. And when these desires meet, we find that our hours are more filled with meaning.

Romans 8:31–39

83

Illumination

Teach me by your Holy Spirit to withdraw my mind from
unprofitable and dangerous inquiries, from difficulties
vainly curious and doubts impossible to be solved.
Let me rejoice in the light which you have imparted.

The gift of simplicity does not call us to shun adventures of the mind and spirit. God, the giver of wisdom, impels us to inquire concerning the mysteries of heavens so vast, of cells so small, of human relations so bewildering. Never to inquire is to rebel against the Mind who works behind our minds, who inspires curiosity and provides some of the means of satisfying it.

Mere adventures, however, can clutter the furnished mental apartments in which we live, can leave cobwebs in the attics of memory, which is the storehouse of intellectual tools. The prayerful life is one that asks for discretion. It is foolish to pose unprofitable and vain questions, such as can the Creator create a rock so heavy that the same Creator cannot move it? These are diversions, human games and nothing more. Such inquirings do not challenge the giant scope of the divine.

Being rid of such idle puzzles does not, however, free us from myriad questions that are *not* beside the point. Yet henceforth we can experience a liberated, focused mind. We ask, How will we put to work the light that, without our even asking for it, insists on shining on our ways today? In the answer to such a question, we learn that there is no doubt that we are called to serve the purposes of God in all our doings: in laboratories, kitchens, nurseries, clinics, offices. In such service, there come ever more answers to ever deeper inquiries.

Ephesians 5:8–14

Orderliness

Turn the works of nature into the works of grace,
by making them orderly, regular, temperate, subordinate,
and profitable to ends beyond their own proper efficacy.

The gift of simplicity minimizes the complications that come with chaos. Let it be agreed that chaos need not always and only confuse and destroy those it surrounds. Quote the scholar who taught that religion is an invention to help people ward off chaos and you can expect a student voice from the back of the classroom to ask, "What's so bad about chaos?" The question echoes philosopher Friedrich Nietzsche, who said that you must have some chaos in your soul to give birth to a dancing star.

Correct though Nietzsche may be for the moments when our poetic leaps are to occur, in practical living whatever is irregular or accidental can become unsettling. It forces earnest people to make their way through brambles of contradictory assignments, jumbles of duties, webs of their own making, and thickets of distraction. At such times they can be paralyzed by the awareness of how chance can produce havoc.

Having tried frantically to master everything, we learn with the wise ones through the ages to open our hands and arms and thus to be free to receive grace. Nature—whether as human nature, Mother Nature's nature, or natural disorder—then becomes transformed. For God, it becomes the raw material with which to recast flaws and faults into graces that serve divine and therefore practical human purposes.

2 Corinthians 5:17–20

Vision

I allow myself to be distracted, when I should be looking steadily at the sun which claims all my attention.

The gift of simplicity offers a blessing of vision. Distractions of daily life can blur our sight, and specters can come to haunt us. Where in this semi-darkness might there be pitfalls? Where might pouncing enemies lie in wait? Eye-catching and alluring trifles also catch our eye, and we lose focus. Where shall we discover the enduring brightnesses we are taught to value?

Whether in shadow or amid glitter, we come to rely on the sun to clarify vision. That gaseous, luminous orb is more to us than a mere physical object 93 million miles away. When unobscured by clouds, it both dispels the dark and turns the glitter pale. The sun also symbolically focuses spiritual impulses, standing as it does for the Creator, who ignited it to dwarf and brighten our globe. Look at the sun, say the mystics, and find your own focus in God.

Look at the sun? Before an eclipse, parents and teachers teach some don'ts to children: Don't look into the sun; you'll become blind. Yet in the last pages of the Scriptures, in Revelation, the seer says, "Then I saw an angel standing in the sun." Such a vision reveals an angel to bring to the mind's eye the things of God. The sun causes the shadows of this day and this night to retreat. Then it illumines the day and exposes the tinsel that ever after begins to look like trash. All that is left for us is the sun with the angel in it.

Revelation 21:22–25

Direction

Let my eyes always look straight ahead on the road you wish me to tread, that I might not be tempted by any distraction.

The gift of simplicity provides the ability to focus, to fix the eye, until the feet can follow. So long as there are distractions or whenever the visual focus wanders, confusion and waywardness result. Of course, it is as easy to say this as it is hard to act upon the insight. Yet to become aware of this is to take a first mental step leading to other steps along the way.

Still: I look at the road that lures me today. How do I concentrate on the straight and narrow path? Over that hill to the left there very well may be underground resources I might mine. On that hill to the right there appears a beacon that sends out signals no adventurer would wish to overlook. Just over this ditch is a fertile field that invites the planter. Over that ditch is a city whose avenues and nooks tease and beckon.

From one corner of the mind comes an implied warning based on experience: only the dullard, it says, sticks to any old road instead of adventuring. From another recess of the brain come new signals that connect with larger worlds that only the obtuse would block out. Unplanted fields, the reminder says, yield harvests of weeds while cities unvisited will leave the passerby deprived of its rewards.

All that brain-prompting fails to note the eye that looks to the road ahead with Christ, who enters our cities and our hearts. Christ calls us to his way. There it is we discern what are mines and where are beacons, to what fields or cities we are called. We will discover what it is that promises and where opportunity beckons. The road God wishes us to tread steadily points toward these.

Matthew 21:1–11

Understanding

O God, help us not despise or oppose
what we do not understand.

The gift of simplicity is never merely what we keep calling it: a gift. To realize itself, it makes demands. The clarity and freedom simplicity promises cannot produce their yield to those whose ignorance or prejudice keeps them from responding. The unknown is terrifying: what is out there, in the stranger's world, that might batter me? It is the unnamed that disturbs. Whatever it is that is hard to believe appears to be poised to attack from the darkness. What is unfamiliar nurtures prejudice. What communities find mildly foreign they soon render atrociously alien. "Stay away from my door, my neighborhood, my country!" cry the owners of intolerant and hateful hearts.

If any of us could face this night or walk into this day saying that we understand everything and despise nothing or that we catch on to everything and find little to oppose, it has to be said that we do not understand. In the world that surrounds us and makes its home within us, there *are* things to despise or oppose. Unopposed, these evils are free to wreak devastations, to perpetuate abuse, to precipitate murder. Literally.

What the gift of simplicity calls forth is an impulse for self-examination. A good question: Do I do my despising and opposing simply because something out there is just too big or too deep or too different for me? There is a better way to be. Learning to see from the viewpoint of the other, conversing to hear his story, all the while beginning to understand—these acts help us sort out and separate the evils we must counter in others from the prejudices that still need facing in ourselves.

Luke 10:25–37

Justice

Grant us grace fearlessly to contend against evil
and to make no peace with oppression; and that we
may reverently use our freedom, help us to employ it
in the maintenance of justice.

The gift of simplicity produces an impulse to support justice. Oppression, its opposite, can look simple. The totalitarianisms in our century and histories of tyrannies past reveal impulses by authorities to efficiently control lives. They would tattoo a serial number in the flesh of victims. They would assemble filing cabinets of information and computer printouts to reinforce their control. Their prison cells would stretch out in long, neat rows.

The closer-up tyranny of the self, *our* self, also appears to take the form of an effort at simplifying. Under it, we do not have to be mindful of manners or customs or laws. "I'll do it my way" is the main hymn of the self-centered culture. Have those who have sung the phrase and acted on it truly achieved simplicity? They have only found that the act of noticing themselves and their interests becomes totally preoccupying. They then lose sight of the needs of others, of situations in which justice should stream forth.

Scholars often note that in the period when republics and democracies were being born, the drafters of constitutions and fighters for freedom assured our rights not so that we could be content with "I can do it my way," but so that we could be responsible citizens. The divine realm is one of greater freedom but never the freedom to serve self-interest alone and thus to increase oppression. This greater freedom permits us, today and tomorrow, to look at the needs of others and thereupon, with clear focus, to follow this vision with works of justice.

Isaiah 42:1–9

Healing

You are the salve that purifies our souls;
you are the ointment that heals our wounds.

The gift of simplicity smooths and heals. Raw and repulsive are the wounds from which we instinctively turn our eyes. Rough is the skin pocked by half-healed injuries. One does not look at many images of mutilation and abrasion without becoming ready to focus on the interior person, to reflect on the raw-rubbed soul.

From the ancients who left records in prescriptions or psalms to modern physicians, healers have recognized that balm, salve, or ointment can cleanse the many wounds of the soul. But applying salve and ointment is less productive than is receiving the gifts and power of the One who does the salving, the anointing. The One who is the anointed, the Messiah, applies the instruments of care and cure. This One is the "You" addressed in prayers old and new. To receive the gifts *of* this You is less rewarding than is receiving the gift that *is* this You.

Wearied souls are purified into newness after receiving such a gift, and old wounds come to be healed. We look today for stories, encounters, and incidents in which the One who offers the healing medication is and remains the healer. We are invited to bring our souls forth in whatever shape they are, with whatever needs they have, that they may be made pure and simple.

Luke 8:40–48

Discipleship

Confound in us, we beseech you, the nice tenderness of our nature, which is averse to that discipline and hardship we ought to endure as disciples of Jesus Christ.

The gift of simplicity includes a call to discipleship. We give and get the wrong impression if we organize our days in an "anything goes" spirit. For believers, living as disciples is not confining, grim, and self-punishing. Instead it inspires the most profound bursts of thanksgiving and an even deeper kind of joy.

The central stories about Jesus reveal the ways he combined a willingness to face hardship, *even unto death*, and invited those who followed him to be ready for their own crosses, burdens lightened by his carrying the heavy end of each. The night before he died, Jesus asked who could undergo what he would in suffering the next day *and* give thanks and speak of the great joy it was to have a sacred meal with those closest to him.

It would be wonderful, wouldn't it, if everything turned out nice, including ourselves and whatever confronts us, once grace comes. But sometimes we can use niceness, goodwill, and pleasant temperaments as barriers against the call of God. The gift of simplicity also is, therefore, a gift that asks for and supports toughness of spirit. With it we are readied for any kind of circumstance, whether nice or marked by hardship. The reason we are thus readied is this: we are henceforth never alone, never bereft of the company of the giver of thanks and joy amid sufferings.

Luke 22:14–20

Reordering

I embrace you, O Lord, because your lowliness
is my greatness, your weakness is my strength,
your foolishness is my wisdom.

The gift of simplicity helps the believer upset all ordinary ways of measuring. We cannot receive or understand this gift, for example, if we keep to the habit of being impressed by ordinary views of what is important and effective. If greatness must imply celebrity and fame, those who seek it become busy with complications along their way. In the end, most will fail. If power means a lure to admire stronger muscles and crave more missiles, people who cherish this will be failed by them. And if wisdom equals world smarts, the wise one will soon and sadly learn the limits of such learning.

Simplicity overturns all those usual ways of thinking and being. Scholars point out that every parable of Jesus is upsetting. In his words in the Gospels, the last shall be first and the first last. The smallest seed becomes the greatest tree. The uninvited receive invitations to the banquet. Those who choose the power seats get pushed under the balcony. The lost sheep and the lost coin count for most. Jesus shows his followers only the way of the cross, wherein the divine power does its saving work through his weakness, his helplessness.

In the forsakenness of Jesus on the cross, his followers come to experience the presence of God. Mention of the cross recalls the divine abandonment, just as the manger of Jesus displays the divine lowliness that disguises but offers greatness. These discernments about the simple ways of God will remain elusive so long as we refuse to deal with the upsetting character of the divine activities. Those activities work in refreshing ways to focus and thus to simplify our lives, our days, this day.

Luke 23:32–49

Transformation

Grant unto your people, that they may love the thing which you command, and desire that which you promise.

The gift of simplicity frees those who experience it from conformity, but it does so by presenting conformity of another sort. To which of the two do we conform? The first entices us to pattern ourselves after the frameworks of the world's strivers, to copy those who invent their own ways and then follow them. The second allows us to be patterned after God in Christ, who graces the world, who offers a way that employs divine creation as the model for everything human.

Can one love what is commanded? A command comes from outside the self and interrupts the way the self would go. Today we would instinctively and stubbornly go our own way, which means the culture's way, seeking our own good and loving it. But toward what end? Those who love what God commands learn that with divine commands come human goods, for God seeks the richest yield for each of us.

How does one come to desire what God promises? This part of the prayer's phrase is easier to cherish than the other, since even the slightest familiarity with the workings of a loving God leads to a faith in the promises. "I will be with you." "I will not leave you comfortless." "I am with you always, even unto the end of the world." "I will give you rest." The objects of ordinary human desire pale when contrasted with what can be heard in the voice of God, the words of Jesus, the stirrings of the Spirit, called the Comforter. Given a hearing, these will transform human love and desire.

John 14:18–21

Hope

*Grant us that having this hope, we may purify ourselves,
even as he is pure; that, when he shall appear again with
power and great glory, we may be made like unto him.*

The gift of simplicity imparts hope. We speak of "having" hope, and even of having "this" hope, a specific hope. For those who walk the way of the cross, behind Jesus, one kind of hope stands out. It is the hope in knowing Jesus as the risen one who promises never to desert us, even beyond physical death. As for finer points, the more profound the thinkers, the less ready they are to dwell on and spell out the detail of what might follow. They will say only that love is stronger than death, that life is not a reality that has to be cramped into our short decades, that we do not have to be content with the limits we now experience, but that we *shall* be "like him," like this risen Christ.

When looking at the visual images of the simple life, most people favor the architecture and furnishings of those who have sought pure line and color and expression—as in wood grains or in window glass. Those who worked with these endeavored lifelong to purify the lines of their tools and their garb. Yet the workers are all gone from us, and their beautiful artifacts will one day fall victim to termites, rust, and decay. The gift of simplicity of which they sang, however, remains a purifying agent to inspire the generations that have followed, that will follow.

The climax of the search for simplicity, the end of the road for followers of the One who gives it as a gift, comes to this: we get to ask that "we may be made like unto him" and that this likeness be a glory that lasts through eternity. This hope, this promise, purifies.

1 Peter 1:3–9

The Photographs

All of the photographs in this book were taken at Shaker Village of Pleasant Hill in Kentucky. Established by the Shakers in 1805, this community was one of several built by early America's largest communal society. The Shakers, although officially known as the United Society of Believers in Christ's Second Appearing, took their name from "Shaking Quakers" (an originally pejorative term the outside world used to describe the whirling dances of the group's worship). Founded by an erstwhile English Quaker, Ann Lee, who came to North America with eight followers in 1774, the movement grew by the 1840s to include several thousand members living in eighteen communities from Maine to Kentucky. Although there were regional differences among them, all subscribed to "Mother Ann's" key convictions, including the importance of living in celibate purity, confessing sins, sharing property, and believing in equality among the races and between the sexes. They set out to create a peaceful way of life, separating themselves from the corrupting influences of the outside world in as many realms as possible. The Shakers have become widely known for their industriousness, inventiveness, fairness, and fine craftsmanship, characteristics that developed from the believers' striving for humility, equality, and simplicity.

Almost every aspect of the Shakers is documented extensively, and there are hundreds of books on the movement; new research is published monthly. Readers wishing to learn more about Shaker crafts, furniture, and architecture would do well to start with any of the many books by June Sprigg. For a highly-acclaimed, thorough account of the Shakers' spiritual roots, history, and legacy, we recommend Stephen J. Stein's *The Shaker Experience in America* (Yale University Press, 1992). Those interested in visiting restored Shaker villages and museums—or the small, still active Shaker community at Sabbathday Lake in Maine— should consult Stuart Murray's comprehensive *Shaker Heritage Guidebook* (Golden Hill Press, 1994).

For more information about visiting Pleasant Hill, contact Shaker Village of Pleasant Hill, 3501 Lexington Road, Harrodsburg, Kentucky 40330-8846, or phone toll-free (800) 734-5411. This village, inhabited by Shakers until 1910, is a National Historic Landmark, with 33 original buildings restored and 2700 acres of farmland preserved. It is the only Shaker site where all visitor services, including dining and overnight lodging, are provided in original buildings.

Notes on the Photographs

The buildings depicted in the photographs were constructed between 1809 and 1860. The names of some of these buildings include "Family," which refers not to a biological family but to one of the five subgroups

The Photographs

made up of several dozen Shakers each who lived and worked together within the larger Pleasant Hill community. Although all scenes and items pictured here can be found at Pleasant Hill, the photographs do not purport to depict only original Shaker artifacts. Because some Shaker communities—including Pleasant Hill—died out decades before their sites were converted to museums, many Shaker artifacts were lost, sold, or destroyed. Consequently, for exhibit and demonstration purposes most of the restored villages have added appropriate period pieces from outside the community, reproductions of surviving Shaker designs, and items that represent educated guesses at long-lost objects for which the appearance cannot be known. It should also be noted that while Pleasant Hill personnel were without exception cordial and helpful during the production of this book, none are responsible in any way for its content, having had no direct involvement in the production or editing of images or text.

Cover — Shaker hat, chair, and broom, Centre Family Dwelling

Frontispiece *(page 2)* — Oval boxes on workbench, East Family Brethren's Shop

Author's Introduction *(page 6)* — Bobbins on scarne, East Family Sisters' Shop

Photographer's Introduction *(page 8)* — Support beams, Carriage House

One Day, One Page *(page 10)* — Berry baskets, Centre Family Dwelling

Attentiveness *(page 13)* — Dorothy cloak in arched hallway, Centre Family Dwelling

Learning *(page 14)* — Schoolroom display, Centre Family Dwelling

Focus *(page 17)* — Cupola, Centre Family Dwelling

Repose *(page 18)* — Cotton-tape chairback, Centre Family Dwelling

*****Community** *(page 21)* — Broom-making supplies, East Family Brethren's Shop

The Sacred *(page 22)* — Meeting House, seen from Centre Family Dwelling

Wisdom *(page 25)* — Beeswax candle-dipping rack, East Family Wash House

Peace *(page 26)* — Main hallway, Centre Family Dwelling

Imagination *(page 29)* — Spiral staircase, Trustees' Office

Freedom *(page 30)* — Gate and latch, East Family farming area

Thresholds *(page 33)* — Worn nailheads in kitchen floorboards, Centre Family Dwelling

*****Church** *(page 34)* — Meeting House

Blitheness *(page 37)* — Wool in basket, East Family Sisters' Shop

Dazzlement *(page 38)* — Dried herbs, Farm Deacons' Shop

Strength *(page 41)* — Ceiling light, West Lot Family Dwelling

Privacy *(page 42)* — Attic, Centre Family Dwelling

Clarity *(page 45)* — Shaker hat, chair, and broom, Centre Family Dwelling

Lodging *(page 46)* — Wall sconce, East Family Dwelling

Asterisks mark Sundays for those who choose to begin this journey on Ash Wednesday and follow it through Lent.

The Photographs

Technical Notes

The photographs were made with view cameras and black-and-white sheet film, mostly 4" x 5" in size. A few were made with 8 x 10 and 11 x 14 film. Each image was printed by the photographer using traditional darkroom techniques.

The Prayers

Most of the prayers that appear with the meditations are excerpts from longer prayers. Here the prayers are listed alphabetically by the first line of the excerpt. Each entry includes the name of the prayer's author and the first line of the prayer from which it was excerpted. Although these prayers can be found in many sources, for general reference we have identified five collections in which these prayers can be found and have noted the appropriate one in each entry. These collections are identified by abbreviations as follows:

> BCP: *The Book of Common Prayer* (Oxford University Press, 1990)
>
> CS: *The Communion of Saints: Prayers of the Famous* (Eerdmans, 1990)
>
> HCBP: *The Harper Collins Book of Prayers: A Treasury of Prayers Through the Ages* (HarperSanFrancisco, 1994)
>
> OXB: *The Oxford Book of Prayer* (Oxford University Press, 1985)
>
> PM: *Praymates: The Days and the Nights & In Joy and in Sorrow* (Thomas More Press, 1993)

"Above all let me live in your presence" *(page 59)* — By St. Thomas Aquinas, c. 1225–1274. From "Loving God, who sees in us." *(HCBP)*

"As the day brings us" *(page 36)* — By Robert Louis Stevenson, 1850–1894. From "O God, as the day returns." *(CS)*

"As the rain hides the stars" *(page 63)* — Gaelic; tr. Alistair MacLean. From "As the rain hides the stars." *(OXB)*

"Be near to me" *(page 16)* — By St. Gertrude, 1256–1302. From "O Love, come to my help." *(PM)*

"Be unto us a comfort on the way" *(page 79)* — The Breviary. From "O God, who didst lead Abraham." *(PM)*

"Confound in us, we beseech you" *(page 99)* — By John Wesley, 1703–1791. From "O God, who by our great Master's example." *(OXB)*

"Enter my room" *(page 43)* — by St. Anselm of Canterbury, c. 1033–1109. From "I am desperate for your love, Lord." *(HCBP)*

"Give me the love of you only" *(page 72)* — By St. Ignatius Loyola, 1491–1556. From "Take, Lord, all my liberty." *(OXB)*

"Give us the spirit of charity" *(page 48)* — By Reinhold Niebuhr, 1892–1971. From "Grant us grace, our Father, to do our work." *(OXB)*

"Give us the true courage" *(page 24)* — By Charles Kingsley, 1819–1875. From "Take from us, O God." *(OXB)*

"God, give us grace to accept" *(page 55)* — By Reinhold Niebuhr, 1892–1971. From "God, give us grace to accept." *(OXB)*

"Grant me to design only what is lawful and right" *(page 75)* — By Samuel Johnson, 1709–1784. From "O God, who hast ordained." *(OXB)*

"Grant that the course of this world" *(page 35)* — The Book of Common Prayer, 1789. From "Grant, O Lord, we beseech thee, that the course of this world." *(BCP)*

"Grant that we may realize" *(page 76)* — By Mary Stuart, Queen of Scotland, 1542–1587. From "Grant that we may realize." *(PM)*

"Grant to us who deal with words and images" *(page 44)* — By David B. Collins, *n.d.* From "God and Father of all." *(OXB)*

"Grant unto your people" *(page 103)* — The Book of Common Prayer, 1789. From "O Almighty God, who alone canst order the unruly wills." *(BCP)*

"Grant us grace fearlessly to contend against evil" *(page 95)* — The Book of Common Prayer, 1789. From "Almighty God, who hast created." *(BCP)*

"Grant us that having this hope" *(page 104)* — The Book of Common Prayer, 1789. From "O God, whose blessed Son was manifested." *(BCP)*

"Guide me to find my rightful place" *(page 56)* — By Jakob Böhme, 1575–1624. From "O God, the source of eternal light." *(HCBP)*

The Prayers

"I allow myself to be distracted" *(page 88)* — By Thérèse of Lisieux, 1873–1897. From "Jesus, you have been very patient with me." *(HCBP)*

"I embrace you, O Lord" *(page 100)* — By St. Aelred of Rievaulx, c. 1110–1167. From "O Lord Jesus, I will embrace you." *(HCBP)*

"Let my eyes always look straight ahead" *(page 91)* — By Jakob Böhme, 1575–1624. From "Rule over me this day." *(HCBP)*

"Let my first thought today" *(page 51)* — By John Baillie, 1886–1960. From "Eternal Father of my soul." *(OXB)*

"Let no little ends" *(page 28)* — By Thomas á Kempis, 1379–1471. From "Almighty God, you who have made all things." *(CS)*

"Let not our minds rest" *(page 12)* — By George Fox, 1624–1691. From "Grant us, O Lord, the blessings of those whose minds are stayed on you." *(CS)*

"Lord, grant me a simple, kind, open, believing, loving, and generous heart" *(page 71)* — By John Sergieff, 1829–1908. From "Lord, grant me a simple, kind, open, believing, loving, and generous heart." *(HCBP)*

"Lord, lift us out of private-mindedness" *(page 64)* — By Bishop Hacket, 17th century. From "Lord, lift us out of private-mindedness." *(PM)*

"Lord, you are like a wildflower" *(page 39)* — By Henry Suso, c. 1295–1366. From "Lord, you are like a wildflower." *(HCBP)*

"Make the threshold of this house" *(page 32)* — St. Stephen's, Walbrook, London. From "O God, make the door of this house." *(PM)*

"May every temporal grace" *(page 80)* — By John Calvin, 1509–1564. From "My God, Father and Savior, since you have commanded us to work." *(HCBP)*

"May he support us all the day long" *(page 47)* — By John Henry Newman, 1801–1890. From "May he support us all the day long." *(OXB)*

"May I know thee more clearly" *(page 68)* — By St. Richard of Chichester, 1197–1253. From "Thanks be to thee, my Lord Jesus Christ." *(PM)*

"O God, help us not despise or oppose" *(page 92)* — By William Penn, 1644–1718. From "O God, help us not despise." *(PM)*

"O God, who hast bound us together" *(page 20)* — By Reinhold Niebuhr, 1892–1971. From "O God, who hast bound us together." *(OXB)*

"Old habits that I cannot throw off" *(page 51)* — From Taiwan. From "Our Father in heaven, I thank thee." *(OXB)*

"Teach me by your Holy Spirit" *(page 84)* — By Samuel Johnson, 1709–1784. From "O Lord, my maker and protector." *(OXB)*

"Teach me, dear Lord" *(page 15)* — By Jean-Pierre de Caussade, 1675–1751. From "You speak, Lord, to all men in general." *(HCBP)*

"Turn my soul into a garden" *(page 52)* — By St. Teresa of Ávila, 1515–1582. From "O Lord my God! I cannot speak." *(HCBP)*

"Turn the works of nature" *(page 87)* — By Jeremy Taylor, 1613–1667. From "O eternal God, who hast made all things." *(OXB)*

"We beseech you to deliver us" *(page 40)* — Akanu Ibaim, Nigeria, *n.d.* From "O Lord, we beseech thee." *(OXB)*

"What a being is ours?" *(page 67)* — By St. Elizabeth Seton, 1774–1821. From "Sweet Lord, what a being is ours?" *(PM)*

"What will befall us today" *(page 83)* — By Princess Elizabeth of France, 1764–1794. From "What will befall us today." *(PM)*

"You are the salve that purifies our souls" *(page 96)* — By Hildegard of Bingen, 1098–1179. From "Holy Spirit, the life that gives us life." *(HCBP)*

"You have through each day" *(page 23)* — By Johann Starck, 1680–1756. From "Gracious God, I praise and thank you." *(HCBP)*

"You made us for yourself" *(page 19)* — By St. Augustine of Hippo, 354–430. From "You awaken us to delight." *(CS)*

"You wove the tapestry of life" *(page 60)* — By St. Clement of Rome, died c. 96. From "You, Lord, brought into being the everlasting fabric." *(HCBP)*

"Your will is our peace" *(page 27)* — By Margaret Cropper, 1886–1980. From "O most blessed Truth." *(OXB)*

Other Books in This Series by Martin and Micah Marty

Places Along the Way: Meditations on the Journey of Faith
matches reflections on the biblical story, from creation to resurrection,
with photographs of the Holy Land.
(Augsburg Fortress, 1994; ISBN 0-8066-2746-8)

Our Hope for Years to Come: The Search for Spiritual Sanctuary
pairs meditations on favorite hymn texts with photographs of North American churches,
from the high Gothic of the city to the rural Gothic of the Plains.
(Augsburg Fortress, 1995; ISBN 0-8066-2836-7)

The Promise of Winter: Quickening the Spirit on Ordinary Days and in Fallow Seasons
combines reflections on psalm texts with images of winter.
(Eerdmans, 1997; ISBN 0-8028-4436-7)

Availability of the Photographs

For permission to reprint or to purchase photographs that appear in *When True Simplicity Is Gained* or any of the above books, please contact

Sterling Black Inc.
60 E. Chestnut, Suite 120
Chicago, IL 60611

Fax: 312.943.0640

E-mail: sterlingbk@aol.com
Web page: www.sterlingblack.com

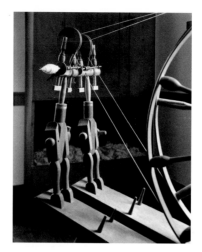

Photographer's Acknowledgments

The author and I once again owe an incalculable debt to Ann Rehfeldt of Sterling Black. Ann serves as editor of text and photos, publishing coordinator, and much much more—from the earliest stages of the conception of these books through the final steps of production and printing. Readers who value the refined art of seamlessly melding photographs and text—the challenge of working with each to complement and enhance the other—will readily understand our appreciation of Ann's considerable talents. Ann's ample skills and experience in the production of art books certainly reveal themselves in projects like this one. We are both very much in her debt.

From my first visit to Pleasant Hill, Larrie Curry, museum director of Shaker Village, grasped the scope and intentions of this project, and she repeatedly went out of her way to help make it a reality. I relied frequently on her expertise in art, history, and management skills, and I cannot picture what I would have done without her generous assistance. Thanks also to Jim Thomas, the president and CEO of Pleasant Hill, and Marcheta Sparrow, director of marketing and public relations, for their support and encouragement of this project. Dixie Huffman, who wears many hats, including that of collections assistant, was a valuable asset, helping with everything from access and logistics to information and historical background. I was also welcomed and assisted in countless ways by the kind members of the Pleasant Hill year-round staff, including Garnett Ashford, Mary Barlow, Connie Carlton, Mac Cecil, Pat Cocanougher, Russell Curtsinger, Randy Folger, Susan Lyons Hughes, Ruth Keller and her friendly colleagues at the front desk, Nooe Long, Martha Sue Mayes, Betty McGrath, Ann Nichols, Edna Quinn, Charla Reed and her helpful associates in the Craft Store, Beverly Rogers, Sheryl Royalty, Ralph Ward, and Mary Lee Woford. Thanks also to the Pleasant Hill housekeeping and maintenance staffs and to Miss Chiff.

This project—including the exhibition of the photographs—would not have been possible without the generous assistance of the Henry Luce Foundation; we are greatly indebted to Henry Luce III, chairman, and John Wesley Cook, president.

Our publisher, Wm. B. Eerdmans, has been most supportive of our books, both before and after publication. The Marty name has appeared on the title page of many Eerdmans books over the years, and we value highly our continuing publishing relationship with them and especially the efforts of Jon Pott, vice president and editor-in-chief.

Finally, it has been our pleasure to work once again with the world leader in printing books of photography, Gardner Lithograph. Gardner's work speaks for itself, but we want to take this opportunity to highlight the particular contributions of David Gray Gardner, Kevin Broady, John Visone, Robert Sweet, and Charles Wright, each of whom played a key role in ensuring the quality of the reproductions. A photographer could not ask for more.